PRAISE FOR

THE MAKING OF A CHAMPION

Indeed, if you find your life caged in the strong champion-making hands of the Almighty God and you are caught between the rock and the hard place in your journey, this powerful Book is for you. The Lord is processing you into a Champion, but you need Apostle Moyo to offer you this knowledge, wisdom and understanding to get you through to the finish line. This Book is needed tool for understanding God's processes with man.

- Dr. Frank Opoku-Amoako, Senior Pastor, Destiny Life International Church, Virginia, USA.

I remember the day I met Josh Moyo sitting at a table in a Denny's Restaurant in Akron, Ohio in 1999. Immediately, I knew I had met a man who will be a friend for lifetime. He and Shirley are two people I have grown to love and have grown just knowing them. Godly...absolutely! They have lived out the strategies of this book following the voice of Jesus as He has led them. Thank you Josh and Shirley for writing your life for all of us to read.

- Pastor David Fisher

Josh Moyo is not just a great preacher but he is a true champion. I say this not just because of his abilities and anointing but because I have seen the brokenness in his inner life. Through personal failures, he has allowed God to mould and craft him into not just into a gifted man but a godly man.

THE MAKING OF A CHAMPION

You will be truly inspired and blessed as you read this book.

- Benny Ho
Senior Pastor of Faith Community Church and President of Arrows College a teaching and Resource Centre for the body of Christ.

The making of a champion is a must have for anyone on a journey to manifest greatness and fulfilling a calling. It's pregnant with practical steps and actions that were taken by the heroes of faith that are bound to make same results as they are timeless principles! It's message is trans-generational and every person can identify with truths in the book. What inspires me the most is not just the David life or the Queen Esther's life which were models, the author himself whom I know personally. He is the reason I am where I am since I desired to emulate him as far back as 1996. He is a true embodiment of the champion he is writing about...

- Apostle Whatmore Makwara.
Founder of Family Worship Centre International Swaziland and President of FWCI School of Ministry, Southern Africa.

The Making of A Champion delves deep into what it takes to overcome and stand strong and mature as a servant of God. Josh Moyo draws from his life and those of great heros of the Bible, to reveal how testing, perseverance, and character position us to advance God's Kingdom and overcome personal obstacles.

As one who has travelled with Josh on the journey, I commend this book as a 'must read'.

- Dr John McElroy
Director, The Southern Cross Association of Churches

God makes strong men, supports them through their suffering and out emerges the strongest of souls. Josh Moyo has experienced this and understands the process.

The making of a champion follows aspects of a life of a misfit to a man God describes "as a man after my own heart."

It will bring hope, healing and help every person to be the champion whom God destined them to be.

- Ian Ballantine
Clinical Psychologist, Armadale District Surgery,
Western Australia

THE MAKING OF A CHAMPION

THE KEY STRATEGIES
OF A CONQUEROR

THE MAKING OF A CHAMPION

THE KEY STRATEGIES OF A CONQUEROR

JOSH MOYO

The Making of a Champion

Copyright © 2018 by Josh Moyo.
All rights reserved.

Requests for information should be addressed to:
joshmoyo@yahoo.com

This book, or parts thereof, may not be reproduced, stored in a retrieval system, or transmitted in any form or by any means, electronic, mechanical, photocopying, recording or otherwise, without the written permission of the publisher.

ISBN 978-0-6482834-6-1

**Published in Australia by
Achiever World Publishers**

ACKNOWLEDGMENTS

Every attempt has been made to credit the sources of copyrighted material used in this book. If any such acknowledgment has been inadvertently omitted or miscredited, receipt of such information would be appreciated

Unless otherwise noted, all scriptures are from the the Holy Bible New King James Version, © 1979, 1980, 1982, 1984 by Thomas Nelson, Inc. Used by permission. All rights reserved.

Scripture quotations marked (NIV) are taken from The Holy Bible, New International Version. Copyright © 1973, 1978, 1984, 2011 by Biblica, Inc.® Used by permission of Zondervan. All rights reserved worldwide. www.Zondervan.com.

DEDICATION

THIS BOOK IS DEDICATED TO THE FOLLOWING:

To my beautiful Parents: Zechariah and Seni: Every accomplishment and achievement in life is a result of the contribution of many people who both directly and indirectly shared their gifts and talents and wisdom with us all. My late father Zechariah and my mum Seni, you have exemplified the ideals of parenthood, you've never moved from your belief in me. Your strength has made me strong. I thank God you shaped and prepared me for my destiny. Words will never express my gratitude.

And to my adopted mum Tiny:
I thank God for the fire in you and your resilience. Most importantly, I thank you for your ability to hear from God. It's that principle that has carried me far. I always desire to hear from

God before I make any decisions. Thank you for the discipline you've instilled in me.

To my beautiful wife Sherley:

Sherley you are my inspiration and my Champion. This book has taken many years to prepare and there were times when it seemed like I would never get through it. Thank you for your support and confidence in me over the many years of marriage. Your endless support, encouragement and persistence helped me to finally complete this work. Many women do noble things, but you surpass them all. On the day you said "I do," you not only said yes to the man, but you also said yes to the assignment God has given me to fulfil. You have proven this over and over in more ways than I can count. Thank you for your unwavering support and unconditional love. I love you, honey

To my two awesome kids, Sharon and Josh Jnr:

You give me the drive to keep striving for more. You have kept your faith in me despite my flaws. As I watch you come into your own, I am prouder and prouder to be your dad. You've been a source of joy and laughter and one of my greatest accomplishments thus far. Even in challenging times, your love for me and God urges me to keep going.

To my spiritual mentors:

Pastor Hans Mashila, who in 1995 embraced me as a son and has never wavered in his role as a father-figure. He did this not only for me but for my wife and kids. That you hold me in the highest esteem is always evident, and your ability to draw out the very best in me has been pivotal in my ministry. Thank you for seeing the gold in this vessel and calling it forth time and time again.

Pastor Merrick Habile, who has always gone out of his way to minister greatness into my life, walks with me without judgment, and always encourages me to be better. You are a father, indeed, a true model of integrity and a great teacher of the Word. Thank you for always encouraging me to look deeper into the Word. You are a treasure to me.

To the Destiny Church Board:

Ian Ballantine, Pastor Merrick Habile, Pastor Mike Bullard, Pastor Lakers Komaiya, Leighton

White, Farai Donhwe, **Blessing Dube, Phil Tonkin, Prince Mukokweza and Trevor Hutchins** for being pillars of strength and reservoirs of wisdom, not just to me but to the entire body of the Destiny Church.

To Phil and Jenny Tonkin: for being part of my journey to restoration, for never losing sight of my potential and reminding me of it often and for being true parental figures to my family and me.

Inonge Muyamwa: for your dedication as my P.A. and Administrator. Many notes, sermons, and media presentations later, your heart has always been to present this ministry with excellence. Most of all, thank you for your faith and trust in me and in the ministry of Destiny over the last 14 years.

To my home church, Destiny Empowered Christian Church

You are the heart of the vision God has given me to fulfil. When I look at you, I see a dream come true, and I look forward with joy and excitement at what's to come.

DEDICATION

And last, but by no means the least, the body of Christ, to whose service I am called. This is for you. I believe in your destiny as much as, if not more, than I believe in my own. Because of God's great love for you, your future is bright. Because of you, this book has true meaning. I am praying that as Paul says, *"The eyes of your understanding will be enlightened; that you may know what is the hope of His calling, what are the riches of the glory of His inheritance in the saints, and what is the exceeding greatness of His power toward us who believe, according to the working of His mighty power which He worked in Christ when He raised Him from the dead and seated Him at His right hand in the heavenly places"* - **(Ephesians 1:18-20).** God bless you. Live out your God-given destiny

CONTENTS

INTRODUCTION
Adversity to Advantage......................................21

CHAPTER 1
What makes a champion? ....…..33

CHAPTER 2
What or who is challenging the
champion in you? ……………………………….…….. 41

CHAPTER 3
Character study: Joseph - the dreaming
champion. …………………………..………………………53

CHAPTER 4
Character study: Samson - honey in a
carcass. …………………………….…………………….. 65

CHAPTER 5
Character study: Esther - the orphaned
queen mother. ……………………………….……….. . 77

CHAPTER 6
Character study: Ruth - resurrecting life
from what's left. 85

CHAPTER 7
Champion's strategy #1: champions are not
born - champions are made. 91

CHAPTER 8
Champion's strategy #2: It takes a champion
 to face another champion. 93

CHAPTER 9
Champion's strategy #3: Champions look
 beyond their abilities. 99

CHAPTER 10
Champion's strategy #4: Champions are
not made by crowds - they are made when
they are alone...103

CHAPTER 11
Confessions of a Champion............................. 107

CONCLUSION
Confessions of a Champion............................. 111

INTRODUCTION

ADVERSITY TO ADVANTAGE

A parable is told of a farmer who owned an old mule. One day, the old mule fell into the farmer's well. The farmer heard the mule praying – or whatever mules do when they fall into wells!

After carefully assessing the situation, the farmer sympathized with the mule but decided that neither the mule nor the well was worth the trouble of saving. Instead, he called his neighbours together, told them what had happened and enlisted them to help haul dirt into the well to bury the old mule and put him out of his misery.

Naturally, at first, the mule was petrified at his imminent demise. However, the farmer and his neighbours continued shovelling dirt on him. Panic-stricken, when the dirt hit him, he immediately shook it off his back. It was at that moment, a thought struck him. It dawned on him that every time a shovel load of dirt landed on his back, he could shake it off and stand on top of it. And that he did! Every time a mound of dirt hit his back, he would shake it off and step up! Blow after blow and mound after mound, he did just that.

ADVERSITY IS YOUR STEPPING STONE

"Shake it off and step up… shake it off and step up… shake it off and step up!" He repeated to encourage himself. No matter how painful the blows or how distressing the situation seemed, the old mule fought panic and just kept right on, shaking it off and stepping up!

> *At the core of every being is the spirit of a conqueror, the spirit of an overcomer.*

It wasn't long before the old mule, battered and exhausted, stepped triumphantly over the wall of that well. What seemed like it would bury him became his stepping stone out of calamity. It all came down to the way he handled his adversity.

That's life! We will face adversity that is so intense it threatens to bury us. However, if we confront our problems, respond to them positively, and refuse to give in to panic, bitterness or self-pity, we will stand a chance of overcoming our trials.

This is true of mankind. At the core of every being is the spirit of a conqueror, the spirit of an overcomer. Winning in life and being the champion in our trials is deeply embedded in us. This comes as part of an original design from our manufacturer.

God says in **Genesis 1:26 (paraphrased)**
"Let us create man in our image and after our likeness and let them have dominion over everything created."

We were created to rule and reign, but we often sell ourselves short. The fear of failure frequently cripples us and causes us to shrink from even trying to go beyond the challenges we face.

DESTINED TO BE A CHAMPION

Each one of us is destined to be a champion. Yes, that's right! You are a champion! That is, God has placed in each of us whatever it will take to conquer, defeat, and annihilate the challenges we are confronted with in our daily walk with God. Regardless of what that challenge may be, how intimidating and menacing it is or whom it may have defeated in the past, God has put in you what it takes to end its reign of terror.

You see, God has a plan for us. Whatever He has to take us through to get us to our destinies, He is well able to do so. He will lead us through it, and through Him, we will conquer anything that stands in our way.

Many of us do not like to deal with our challenges because they can be very unpleasant and intimidating.

> *Many of us do not like to deal with our challenges because they can be very unpleasant and intimidating.*

However, we need to realize that at one time or another, each of us will be forced to deal with the ones that confront us daily. Some days, we may have avoided conflict or even taken flight as we ran from our challenges, but the plain truth is we simply cannot avoid them forever. They are not going to stand still and refuse to act against us. Rather, they will actively attempt to destroy us. They will try to haunt us for years, take over our territory, and paralyse us with fear. They will not simply vanish and go away.

KNOW THE STRATEGIES OF THE ENEMY

Challenges come in various forms, in many ways, and they affect all of us differently based on the experiences of our lives and varied backgrounds. One of the strange things about challenges is that they can be extremely personal in nature. What may haunt and torment one person may be a small stepping stone or a midget to someone else who can quickly and easily dispose of it. It is all a matter of perspective.

As a matter of fact, the challenges the Enemy uses against us are usually specifically designed and programmed to battle us in our areas of weakness and fear. He will use our past and life traumas to design a demon that will attack us in our weak spots. He will use the lure of popularity to get us involved in activities we know we shouldn't be in, so we can try to be with the in-crowd. He will bring men or women with bad intentions into our lives. He will use them to pull us down as we try to fill the void left by our absent fathers or mothers. He will disguise drugs and alcohol as ways to escape our emotional anguish during a season of struggle. He will use sex to tempt us into believing it will help us feel better about ourselves as we try to heal our low self-image.

YOU CAN OVERCOME YOUR GIANTS

When the Enemy does these things, he intensifies his attacks by playing on our greatest fears: fear of abandonment, fear of not being accepted by our friends, fear of being alone or fear of surrendering and following God. All of these fears are giants: giants of peer pressure, giants of sexual temptation, giants of family struggle, giants of poverty, giants of academic challenges, as well as giants of unforgiveness and bitterness. The Enemy uses these types of giants to cause our walk with God to be filled with discomfort and to haunt us through the night. The fact of the matter is that most of the giants we fear never really materialise anyway. Yet, they are giants nonetheless. However, I believe God is raising champions in these last days, and all of us are destined to be champions.

The Word of God is full of stories of conquests in which God uses the least likely individuals to accomplish His purpose. He used people who would most likely have never dreamed they would be champions. In His wisdom and providence, God ordained it to be so.

The words spoken by God in Jeremiah 29:11 have significantly moulded my thinking. He says He has plans to prosper us, plans of hope and plans for a good future.

BEHIND EVERY GLORY, THERE IS A STORY

I grew up in a loving family, but we didn't have much material wealth or resources. It was challenging. Consequently, I developed a belief that winning in life or being a champion was reserved for others, not me. I often settled for the bottom of the barrel in many things, and I unwittingly reinforced my belief that life should serve me the dregs of everything.

I am one of a set of twins, raised in a family of 10 siblings, 5 boys and 5 girls. Tragically, my twin brother lost his life after sustaining a snake bite at the age of 6, which was devastating, to say the least. Nonetheless, my upbringing was happy and wholesome, but it was not glamorous or fancy by any standards. In addition to this, I was born in a country that has suffered economic and civil unrest for a long time. Admittedly, this is not something that one notices as prominently as the outside onlooker. In our time, we just, as they say, "got on with it."

My father was a miner in Shabanie (Zvishavane), an industrial town known for its asbestos mining. This is where I started all my schooling, from primary all the way up to secondary education. I used candles or kerosene lamp light to study because there was no electricity. Once again, that was normal for me. The asbestos mining in Shabanie, though it was a small town, gave it much of its prominence and infrastructure. Hence, many migrated there in search of employment. My father was one who moved with his family to live in the town. As my father had not received much formal education, this impacted the pay grade at which he could work and understandably placed him a lower socio-economic bracket. The level of housing and amenities he could afford for his family was determined by his income.

> *I was born in a country that has suffered economic and civil unrest for a long time.*

Once I reached a certain age in my schooling, the elements of life that were once quite normal for me began to stand out. I was confused that my friends had homes with electricity and running water – and don't even let me get started on packed lunches. I found myself not wanting to open my lunch in the presence of my friends because my lunch was a bit off and not your typical midday school lunch.

It would be untrue if I told you this didn't bother me. As a young teenager, times were much the same as they are now. Peer pressure and the need to fit in were major factors in our lives. My stale lunches and sometimes worse-for-wear uniforms did nothing to help with this! I still remember quite vividly countless times when the school registrar would walk from class to class looking for students whose school fees had not been paid to take them out of their lessons. I would instinctively pack my books without waiting for my name to be called because I was often at the top of that list. These instances affected how I viewed myself and, in turn, who I chose to associate with. My impression of who I was and what God intended for me had been significantly marred.

Humans are born with a great need to be loved and to have a sense of belonging and security.

My home life was a very good one. My father always assured and reinforced in all his children that we were valuable despite the conditions we were in. My school was an entirely different story that brought my self-image and esteem down quite significantly. I struggled constantly to remain afloat with what I knew to be true – what my father said about me versus what I could see in the natural. Why am I sharing all this? I am sharing all this to say you cannot change your history. You cannot change where you were born. However, you can change where you are and where you are going.

THE CHAMPION WITHIN

The champion in me was stirred by my father. He would speak to all his children every morning before we went to school. He would tell us we could achieve all we set our minds to. That we could achieve all the great things we applied ourselves to and focused on. Consequently, I was roused with great determination and belief that my life would change for the better. I meditated and repeated my father's words when I was on my own. He would tell me, "You are somebody." "Your environment does not define who you are." "You are better than what you are presently going through."

I was so impacted by my father's encouragements that when I saw an aeroplane in the sky, I would point at it and say, "Hey aeroplane! One day, you will carry me all over the world!" This was so much like second nature to me, that one time I uttered the exact words forgetting my friends were within earshot. Of course, they laughed at me mercilessly! As if to say, "Josh, your shirt is literally hanging onto your body by its last shreds; you don't even have a bicycle. What aeroplane plans are you imagining?" I learnt from that experience your beliefs and your convictions can only be sustained by the one who has placed them in you to begin with. With all humility, I can testify of God's faithfulness to His Word. I have had the awesome privilege of ministering the gospel in over 35 countries worldwide. Public opinion will not define your destiny or your destination. That is between you and God.

> *"You are better than what you are presently going through."*

I got saved at the age of 11, but my realisation of the richness and abundance available in Christ took some time to eventuate. I was surrounded by the spirit of religion and the influences of people who did not know much as far as pursuing and knowing God was concerned. I thank God that early on in my journey; I was invited to attend a conference where Jeremiah 29:11 was preached. The preacher emphasised that the great plans God had for me could only be revealed to me by the Holy Spirit.

Boy was I ready for those plans! I remember thinking whoever this Holy Spirit is, I want Him! I was first in line at the altar call that day, and in that moment, my view of myself was transformed forever.

> *Public opinion will not define your destiny or your destination.*

My prayer is that as you read this book, the spirit of championship will be stirred within you. All that has been defeating you will now take on a different shape. You will see yourself rising triumphantly out of your challenges by the power of Jesus Christ. You are a CHAMPION.

CHAPTER 1

WHAT MAKES A CHAMPION?

There are core characteristics and traits that make a champion and our main character throughout this book, David, possessed them. His life was not smooth or perfect but that alone tells me how challenges mould the champion in us. Our text tells us how David rose to be one of the greatest influencers of his time.

Our journey begins in the 1 Samuel chapter 17. This ancient narrative has been shared over and over but still holds its power today.

That is the great thing about the Word of God; you can never over-preach it. Every time you read the Word of God, you can receive new revelations that will help you move along on your journey with God.

Our text covers a time in the life of David, who rose from obscurity, simply tending his father's sheep to be a great warrior, Israel's king, and a pivotal character in the tapestry of God's divine plan.

"And all the men of Israel, when they saw the man, fled from him and were dreadfully afraid. So, the men of Israel said, "Have you seen this man who has come up? Surely, he has come up to defy Israel; and it shall be that the man who kills him the king will enrich with great riches, will give him his daughter, and give his father's house exemption from taxes in Israel." Then David spoke to the men who stood by him, saying, "What shall be done for the man who kills this Philistine and takes away the reproach from Israel? For who is this uncircumcised Philistine, that he should defy the armies of the living God?"

And the people answered him in this manner, saying, "So shall it be done for the man who kills him. - (1 Samuel 17:24-27).

The word "champion" is defined in different ways, but a simple way to explain it is "one who defies and wins despite obstacles and keeps winning."

WHAT MAKES A CHAMPION?

SPEAK VICTORY

Muhammad Ali is a great picture of a champion. We can all identify him as boxing's most celebrated athlete and heavyweight champion. No matter whom he came up against, no matter how tall his opponent was, he continued to speak his victory.

I often wonder why as Christians, we don't learn the principle that the words we speak are, indeed, powerful. What you say *to* yourself is powerful. What you say *about* yourself is powerful. Muhammad Ali was known for many charismatic phrases,

> *What you say about yourself is powerful.*

"I'm young. I'm handsome. I'm fast. I can't possibly be beat."

"I am the greatest. I said that even before I knew I was."

That's how champions talk.

So our narrative in 1 Samuel 17 confirms the very same thing. We know already that we are not fighting for our victory. The victory is already won. We are fighting from a position of victory because Jesus Christ has already done the hard yards for us. He has fought our battles and because of this, you and I are victorious.

So, ladies and gentlemen, when we talk about the making of a champion, it's important to understand that in the normal set up of life, this entails facing many stresses and challenges. Often, these challenges come at times when we are completely unprepared. But if we keep our focus on Jesus and remember that He is on our side, the journey we travel is one of ultimate victory. God can do anything for us.

The story we have just read talks about a battle that is fought between two mountains. On one side, we have the children of Israel and on the other, we have the Philistines. The Philistines have a character in their camp called Goliath. We are told by the scriptures that he is a local champion from the land of Gath. This formidable character busies himself for 40 days taunting and speaking words of intimidation to the children of Israel. He is out and out defying God's people and cursing their God in the name of his gods.

As he does this, he asks for the children of Israel to do one thing – send one person from their camp to fight him. The condition is the victor gets to reign over the one defeated. The

WHAT MAKES A CHAMPION?

challenge is on. Saul's camp faces this battle against a company of giants. What does Saul do? He offers some incentives to his military saying, "Whoever fights the giant Goliath and wins, receives a lifetime tax-free exemption and the king's daughter as a reward."

We're told in the scriptures that when the men in Israel heard about Goliath, his big stature and equally big talk, they fled! Personally, I don't blame them. By all accounts, Goliath was a big guy! But if you'll allow me to say to you dear reader, you are not designed to run away from your enemy. More directly, you are not designed to run away from the devil. You are not designed to run away from circumstances that are opposing you. You're meant to face them like the warrior you are. With God on your side, you are more than a conqueror.

> *You are not designed to run away from circumstances that are opposing you.*

You might be thinking at this point, what should I do if I have opposition on every side. I feel outnumbered. I feel ill-equipped and hopeless. I'm told I am a champion but I feel like anything but a champion. I declare to you that winning battles is not about size but about strategy.

NO ONE IS EXEMPT

We have already established that none of us are immune to the challenges, struggles, and stresses of life. No one is exempt; we will all at one time or another face trials and hardships. We will all encounter problems.

It is my prayer that by the time you have finished reading this book, you will be able to face these challenges, not with confidence in yourself and your abilities but with confidence in God. He stands with you and gives you the strength and wisdom to face every giant in your life.

What is your current situation? What are your current circumstances? Whose voice shouts the loudest in your ears? Through what lenses do you view yourself? What is holding you back from living to your full potential? Is it past mistakes, unhappiness about your present circumstances or perhaps fear of the future?

WHAT MAKES A CHAMPION?

Paul the apostle reminds us that nothing shall separate us from the love of God **(Romans 8:35-39).**

Who shall separate us from the love (agape) of Christ? Shall tribulation, or distress, or persecution, or famine, or nakedness, or peril, or sword?
- (Romans 8:35).

Paul is reminding us that nothing can arrest or deny the resurrection of the champion in you except yourself. Regardless of what they are facing, champions rise above it. They rise above adversity and do what they are born to do. A basketball in the hand of Michael Jordan unmasked the champion in him. Itzhak Perlman's violin is his champion-making tool.

One of the hardest questions we may ask ourselves, but one that begs to be asked and demands answering is, "Why are you here?" You might ask this question during an amazing opportunity or you may feel the need to ask it after having made the worst mistake of your life. Nonetheless, answering this question is the only way to unlock the champion in you.

Growing up in my village in Zimbabwe, answering the question "Why am I here?" helped me see my destination was greater than my origin. It helped me see I was greater than the place of my birth.

Remember, it is not all smooth sailing once you make the decision to ignite your champion spirit. Fear rises in you when you take this bold step. "What if people don't approve of me?" "What if they can't see in me what I see in myself?" are thoughts that may fill your mind. However, you can't let this stop you! Instead, brave the negative reactions and criticisms.

Live to your true self. Never allow people's approval to prevail over self-approval, and most importantly, God's approval. Living according to people's expectations and their approval will only result in a life of mediocrity. Discover what God has invested in you.

> *Remember, it is not all smooth sailing once you make the decision to ignite your champion spirit.*

CHAPTER 2

WHAT OR WHO IS CHALLENGING THE CHAMPION IN YOU?

When we first hear of David, we know him to be a young, ruddy, sheep boy. There is nothing much to mention about him and nothing exciting or inspiring that even makes us see him as a champion.

We are told that David is the youngest of all his brothers who are physically big, strapping lads. David's story begins when his people, the Israelites, are being threatened by an enemy.

Of all the enemies Israel faced, few are as famous or as menacing as the Philistine giant of Gath named Goliath, whose name means splendour. His height was "six cubits and a span," which would make him ten and a half feet tall.

The army of Israel had been in conflict with the Philistines for many years and here, in one of their many battles, they are challenged by a warrior who was incomparable to anyone they had seen before. He stood as Israel's worst nightmare taunting and haunting them for forty days. But God raised the most unlikely of challengers to conquer this giant who defied the armies of the living God.

Let's take a look at David, the shepherd boy, the young boy destined to be a giant killer. Let us see how God would use him to conquer Israel's worst enemy despite the problems working against him. We will discuss David the Disadvantaged, David the Prepared, and David the Victorious.

DAVID THE DISADVANTAGED

Many times, the picture we get of David during his years as a shepherd boy is a wonderful and pleasant one. We imagine him sitting in a field, surrounded by sheep, playing his harp and peacefully writing new songs. Let me suggest to you that this was not the case at all, but it was actually a painful time for David.

David was the rejected son.

David's father Jesse was blessed with many sons; David was the youngest. It was the custom and belief of the day that the father of a household was the carrier of a blessing. His words and approval were intended to propel a son toward his destiny.

We are told the story of how the prophet Samuel came to town to anoint the next king and Jesse lined up all his big strong sons. He was certain that the next king of Israel was among them. Sadly, David did not make the cut because of his appearance, and he was left out in the pasture. David did not even receive mention or acknowledgement. I am being honest with you: if that was me, I would feel worthless and rejected. It was a clear message from David's own father that he did not consider him to be a man of substance, certainly, not enough substance to bring him before the one who anoints kings.

I can imagine the void it left in David and how undervalued he would have felt by his own father. Statistics tell us that the Absent Father Syndrome is in 48 per cent of homes. We find that either these homes have no physical father-figure or the father is present but does not fulfil the duties a father should.

It's clear to me that David's brothers learnt from their father's example because, at the time of the anointing, none of the brothers spoke up to say, "Hey Dad, you've forgotten David!"

I am grateful though that God has a way of selecting what man rejects. He uses the things that man would ordinarily cast aside as useless and turns them into mighty instruments for His glory.

I can think of many social misfits that God used:

1. A fugitive like Moses
2. A conman like Jacob
3. A wanderer like Abraham
4. A dreamer like Joseph
5. A prostitute like Rahab
6. A poor boy like Gideon
7. A tax collector like Zacchaeus

It encourages me to know that I don't have to be perfect or palatable to man for God to use me. It creates a sense of relief and hope that even with my flaws, inadequacies, and failings, there is a champion brewing inside me.

God used David's sense of isolation to develop a longing for him and dependency on God. This is the position God wants us in. When we learn the value of relying on God for our strength, we will never lack the stamina to finish the assignment He has given us. All the grace we need is found in Him and in Him, we are always sufficient.

David is known to have penned many writings that showed the position of his heart towards God:

"When my father and my mother forsake me then the Lord will take me up." - **(Psalm 27:10).**

"Some trust in Chariots, some trust in horses but we will remember the name of the Lord" - **(Psalm 20:7).**

Now the story continues with David as he shows up on the scene to deliver lunches to his brothers. You will notice their responses:

"Then David spoke to the men who stood by him, saying, "What shall be done for the man who kills this Philistine and takes away the reproach from Israel? For who is this uncircumcised Philistine, that he should defy the armies of the living God?"

And the people answered him in this manner, saying, "So shall it be done for the man who kills him."

Now Eliab his oldest brother heard when he spoke to the men; and Eliab's anger was aroused against David, and he said, "Why did you come down here? And with whom have you left those few sheep in the wilderness? I

know your pride and the insolence of your heart, for you have come down to see the battle."
- **(1 Samuel 17:26-28).**

DAVID THE PREPARED

Whatever our destinies are, God has a way of taking us through things to prepare us for the next level. The greater the investment and the giftedness, the greater the struggle and the season of preparation is going to be. *"For unto whomsoever much is given, of him shall be much required"*
- **(Luke 12:48).**

Shepherding was the job no one else wanted. In fact, all of the young boys wanted to be warriors. Being a shepherd certainly wasn't appealing. It was an all-weather job, come rain, shine or snow, the shepherd was out in the pasture shovelling dung and chasing after sheep. He would fight off wolves and predators. I'll bet you David did not know that God had him in training.

The Bible tells us of many encounters David had that showed his time in the fields was not in vain. God was preparing him for something greater. When it came time to face the giant,

King Saul made a very good point about David's credentials:

And Saul said to David, "You are not able to go against this Philistine to fight with him; for you are a youth, and he a man of war from his youth."

Suddenly all those precarious nights in the fields made sense to David and he replied:

But David said to Saul, *"Your servant used to keep his father's sheep, and when a lion or a bear came and took a lamb out of the flock,*

I went out after it and struck it, and delivered the lamb from its mouth; and when it arose against me, I caught it by its beard, and struck and killed it.

Your servant has killed both lion and bear; and this uncircumcised Philistine will be like one of them, seeing he has defied the armies of the living God."

Moreover David said, "The Lord, who delivered me from the paw of the lion and from the paw of the bear, He will deliver me from the hand of this Philistine." And Saul said to David,

"Go, and the Lord be with you!"
- (1 Samuel 17:33-37).

God used the lion and the bear to prepare David for the giant. You may be facing lions and bears in your life right now:

- Lions and bears of rejection
- Lions and bears of depression
- Lions and bears of heartache and past life traumas
- Lions and bears of low self-esteem
- Lions and bears of unpopular choices
- Lions and bears of family problems
- Lions and bears of poverty
- Lions and bears of parental divorce

To you I say, do not despise your hardships. They are your preparation for what is ahead. Challenges can be exhausting for everyone, to say the least. As we go through them, it is hard to see their purpose, but David's story teaches me that there is a purpose in my struggle. There is a reason for my afflictions.

DAVID THE VICTORIOUS

Using His Own Weapons

So Saul clothed David with his armour, and he put a bronze helmet on his head; he also clothed him with a coat of mail.

David fastened his sword to his armour and tried to walk, for he had not tested them. And David said to Saul,

"I cannot walk with these, for I have not tested them." So David took them off. **-(1 Samuel 17:38- 39).**

A valuable lesson we learn from David is that he learnt the value of using his own weapons. David's stones were designed specifically for him. He could not use Saul's armour, and Saul could not work those stones. A message is embedded here. We all have our armour exclusively given to us by God. Each of us is unique, so be the best version of yourself, not a cheap imitation of someone else. Many of us scorn what God has gifted us. We think it's not good enough to work with, but it will surprise you what God can use.

- Moses used a rod

- Samson used the jawbone of an ox

- He used Shunammite woman's cake to sustain a prophet

- Elijah used an axe-head

 - Solomon's wisdom

 - John the Baptist's fire

 - Mary's womb

- A pot of water at a wedding

- A little boy's lunch

- Mud mixed with spit

- The hem of a garment

- Peter's zeal and passion

- Paul's intellect

- John's Revelation

Champions know the weapons set aside for them. It's not how big and fancy the weapon is; it's not how heavy the weapon is. It is the knowledge of the one wielding the weapon that makes it mighty in battle.

"Then he took his staff in his hand; and he chose for himself five smooth stones from the brook, and put them in a shepherd's bag, in a pouch which he had, and his sling was in his hand. And he drew near to the Philistine." **-(1 Samuel 17:40).**

Perhaps you have put away your weapon because you didn't think it was significant. If you did, it is time to go back to the river brook where the water of the Holy Spirit has been washing over and anointing it. Pick it up again! Go back and pick up your weapon!

IN THE NAME OF THE LORD

One of the most fundamental lessons a champion will learn is that all he does is in the name of the Lord.

Then David said to the Philistine, *"You come to me with a sword, with a spear, and with a javelin. But I come to you in the name of the Lord of hosts, the God of the armies of Israel, whom you have defied. 46 This day the Lord will deliver you into my hand, and I will strike you and take your head from you. And this day I will give the carcasses of the camp of the Philistines to the birds of the air and the wild beasts of the earth, that all the earth may know that there is a God in Israel -* **(1 Samuel 17:45, 46).**

Are you thinking what I'm thinking? We all know David's stature, so it is fair to say that this is BIG TALK coming from such a small fella! But David knew whose name he bore. Champions know whose strength they are drawing from. David knew whose assignment he was fulfilling. It was God's limitless strength. When David made this declaration, he was drawing from an endless supply of strength and power, which far outweighed his opponent's weapons and strength.

CHAPTER 3

CHARACTER STUDY JOSEPH: THE DREAMING CHAMPION

I operate under the philosophy that champions are made as opposed to them being born. They are made by their circumstances – good and bad. They are made by what challenges them. They are made by the very things that threaten to kill them. Instead of giving up, they rise to life's challenges and face them head-on.

I know that champions are made because the Bible tells me a story about a young lad named Joseph whose introduction to success was stormy, filled with pain and episodes in prison. Yet, overnight, his story was transformed and his location changed to a palace. Before we get ahead of ourselves, let's be reminded of his story found in **Genesis 37:**

Now Jacob dwelt in the land where his father was a stranger, in the land of Canaan. This is the history of Jacob. Joseph, being seventeen years old, was feeding the flock with his brothers. And the lad was with the sons of Bilhah and the sons of Zilpah, his father's wives; and Joseph brought a bad report of them to his father.

Now Israel loved Joseph more than all his children, because he was the son of his old age. Also he made him a tunic of many colours. But when his brothers saw that their father loved him more than all his brothers, they hated him and could not speak peaceably to him.

Now Joseph had a dream, and he told it to his brothers; and they hated him even more. So he said to them, "Please hear this dream which I have dreamed: There we were, binding sheaves in the field. Then behold, my sheaf arose and also stood upright; and indeed, your sheaves stood all around and bowed down to my sheaf." And his brothers said to him, "Shall you indeed reign over us? Or shall you indeed have dominion over us?" So they hated him even more for his dreams and for his words. **- (Genesis 37:1-8).**

"TALL POPPY SYNDROME."

This picture painted for us during our first introduction to Joseph gets me every time. Here is a young man whose early life is characterised by favour. He is his father's favourite, and this causes some animosity with his siblings. You will agree with me that this is a normal occurrence even in modern-day reality. Sometimes, extraordinary favour in our lives can bring the disdain and jealousy of others.

One would expect that where there is a reason to celebrate the success of another, celebration would be the most natural response.

> *Sometimes, extraordinary favour in our lives can bring the disdain and jealousy of others.*

However, Joseph's brothers did what many people do when they feel "passed over" for promotion. They try to pull the promoted one down. I've heard of it referred to as the "tall poppy syndrome." This says, "You might be up there now, but it doesn't make you better than anyone else. In fact, we had better cut you down to size before you get any delusions of grandeur." And cut down they did. The story tells us that Joseph's brothers ridiculed him with their words when he shared his flamboyant and boisterous dream.

I always chuckle to myself when I read what happens next because it's evident that Joseph is not perturbed by his siblings' scorn. Instead, he goes on to share his second dream, which is even more grandiose than the first.

Then he dreamed still another dream and told it to his brothers, and said, "Look, I have dreamed another dream. And this time, the sun, the moon, and the eleven stars bowed down to me." So he told it to his father and his brothers; and his father rebuked him and said to him, "What is this dream that you have dreamed? Shall your mother and I and your brothers indeed come to bow down to the earth before you?" And his brothers envied him, but his father kept the matter in mind **- (Genesis 37:9-11 NKJV).**

PROTECT YOUR DREAM

Now, it's clear here that there is something phenomenal about our man Joseph. It's undeniable, God is working in him and something is brewing within him, but perhaps because of his immaturity, he makes what I would call a "classic rooky mistake" – too much, too soon. He shares what God is saying to him and expects celebration, but instead, he gets condemnation. Can you identify? I'm sure you've heard it said before, "Not everyone will be happy for your success." Joseph experienced this first hand and we know the story well. His brothers plot against him, and he finds himself in a tailspin that no one would want to be in.

> *"Not everyone will be happy for your success."*

Instead of being celebrated for this role, Joseph is subjected to a fate you would not wish on your worst enemy and at the hands of his own blood relatives. He is condemned to die. Why? That is the first question that goes through my head. Joseph meant well. He was a young man with big dreams, high hopes and a love for his family. But in an instant, those high hopes were ripped from him. He was beaten, shoved into a deep pit and left for dead. The story goes on to tell us, the only act of mercy in Joseph's life was when one of his brothers spared his life and sold him to foreign traders. His life was spared but really, it seems like an out of the frying pan into the fire situation because Joseph would have surely felt great pain and rejection.

Joseph's afflictions didn't stop at him being sold to outsiders. His brothers went on to tell his father that he was dead and funeral arrangements were even made. Are you picturing it with me?

Imagine your siblings telling your father you were killed when you are still alive.

BURRIED ALIVE

Joseph's brothers took word to their father that wild animals had eaten him. And Jacob mourned the loss of his favourite son. In his deep sorrow, he buried Joseph (who is alive) in the deep recesses of his heart. Joseph might as well have been dead! But what Jacob, and I daresay, Joseph did not know at the time, is that this is how champions are made.

> *Don't put a full stop on something God has only put a comma on.*

It's not over until God says it's over. Don't put a full stop on something God has only put a comma on. Has the joy of life been ripped from you? Have you had the worst life has to offer thrown at you? Has all the hope of life been sucked out of you? Everything in your life may seem dead, but it's not the end of your story.

The story goes on to tell us of the many hurdles and hardships Joseph faced but eventually, justice found him, and God's plan was realised.

The LORD was with Joseph, and he was a successful man; and he was in the house of his master the Egyptian. And his master saw that the LORD was with him and that the LORD made all he did to prosper in his hand. So Joseph found favour in his sight, and served him. Then he made him overseer of his house, and all that he had he put under his authority. So it was, from the time that he had made him overseer of his house and all that he had, that the LORD blessed the Egyptian's house for Joseph's sake; and the blessing of the LORD was on all that he had in the house and in the field. Thus he left all that he had in Joseph's hand, and he did not know what he had except for the bread which he ate. Now Joseph was handsome in form and appearance
- (Genesis 39:2-6).

GLIMPSE OF DESTINY

Joseph had a glimpse into his destiny many times, but the steps to its fulfilment were generously peppered with ups and downs. He had to face the hatred of his family because of the magnitude of the destiny within him. He had to endure estrangement from his beloved father because his was not an ordinary course of travel. He had to defy seemingly insurmountable odds – and defy them, he did!

The making of the champion in Joseph began early in his life. God showed him the preview of his destiny through the two significant dreams we've read about. The very dreams he shared with his family. Both times, his family ridiculed him. If only they knew the role Joseph would play in their salvation during times of famine and hardship down the line.

Joseph's life with all its ups and downs teaches me a few things that characterise true champions.

DON'T BE AFRAID TO DREAM BIG

One thing we must keep foremost in our minds is that God has invested a lot in each of us. That means that in this race of life, we all have a role to play, and we must play it well. Many of us have become content with living mediocre lives. We are content with simply "getting by." But Joseph dreamt big. Even when he was ridiculed, scorned, and almost killed for his dreams, he held them close to his heart. Maybe, you're like

Joseph. Instead of people celebrating your great ideas, they spit on them and push you to the side. Nevertheless – keep on dreaming!

DON'T GET DISTRACTED

We know that after Joseph was sold to the Midianites, he experienced temporal amnesty from his predicaments. Yes, it had been nightmare after nightmare up until that point, but that familiar favour seemed to be making a reappearance into Joseph's life. Potiphar appointed him as an overseer to his household. Things were looking mighty good until Potiphar's wife was sucked into the undeniable pull of the favour on Joseph's life.

To you, dear champion in the making, I will say this: "Favour attracts." The trouble is favour attracts both good and bad. We would love if the favour God has placed on our lives would only attract the beneficial but unfortunately, it attracts everything – flies and all. Don't get distracted. Know that you have a real enemy of your destiny. He's trying to prevent your destiny from being fulfilled and seeing the champion in you rising up. It can be tempting to give up and go with the flow, to go with what's easier, but resist anything that does not line up with the direction of your destiny.

PREPARE FOR PRISON

Let me be very honest with you, if I were Joseph, by now, I would have been petitioning God on his methods. First, Joseph is rejected by his family for sharing his perfect dreams. If that was not enough, he was thrown into jail even though he did nothing wrong. He did the right thing and fled from Potiphar's wife. Talk about confusing! Joseph literally spent 14 years in jail for a crime he didn't commit! For many years, he must have felt abandoned and cheated by God. But Joseph persisted and even in jail, that persistent favour in his life resurfaced.

When the favour of God is on your life, you can be sure of His presence and prosperity in all you do. I think of God's favour in the life of a champion as sponsorship that never elapses. Regardless of your location or

> *God values you as his star player. He will protect his investment in you without fail.*

circumstances, God values you as his star player. He will protect his investment in you without fail. Even in the dark moments when he was forgotten by everyone he trusted, God showed Joseph His favour, so much so, that even prison was a platform for the champion in Joseph to come forth.

P.I.T. = PRIME MINISTER IN TRAINING

After years of being forgotten, Joseph gets out of prison and is elevated to the highest office in the land. This is where the fun really begins. We see the push and pull that most champions encounter at one time or another in their lives. At some point in your life, you will realise that everything you have been through was a preparation for a greater purpose.

> *At some point in your life, you will realise that everything you have been through was a preparation for a greater purpose.*

When Joseph is placed face-to-face with the people who plotted evil against him, he has a big choice to make. The Bible tells us that all the pain he was subjected to by his family comes flooding back to him in a moment of deep despair. Joseph remembers the pit, the palace, Potiphar's wife, and prison.

Finally, as he stands in the role of prime minister, he has to decide at this point to either make his aggressors pay or save them and be the champion he was called to be in the first place. I thank God for the champion in Joseph because it encourages me to pick the latter.

Life can hit me with its best shot, throw me in a pit, leave me for dead, sell me like I'm worthless, falsely accuse me and forget me but if I hold on to the investment of championship in me, I will be able to utter Joseph's famous words, *"What was meant for evil, God has turned around for good."*

CHAPTER 4

CHARACTER STUDY SAMSON: HONEY IN A CARCASS

I know that champions are made because of the story of a mighty man named Samson.

His story is found in **Judges 14:1-8**.

Samson was on a special mission to get a wife in a place called Timnah. The background story is that God sought a way to defeat the Philistines and Samson was going to be the catalyst for this victory.

The story tells us that Samson pursues this path despite internal (family) and external (society and the environment) opposition.

So, the story goes:

Now Samson went down to Timnah and saw a woman in Timnah of the daughters of the Philistines. So he went up and told his father and mother, saying,

"I have seen a woman in Timnah of the daughters of the Philistines; now therefore, get her for me as a wife."

Then his father and mother said to him, "Is there no woman among the daughters of your brethren, or among all my people, that you must go and get a wife from the uncircumcised Philistines?" And Samson said to his father, "Get her for me, for she pleases me well."

But his father and mother did not know that it was of the LORD--that He was seeking an occasion to move against the Philistines. For at that time the Philistines had dominion over Israel. So Samson went down to Timnah with his father and mother, and came to the vineyards of Timnah.

Now to his surprise, a young lion came roaring against him. And the Spirit of the LORD came mightily upon him, and he tore the lion apart as one would have torn apart a young goat, though he had nothing in his hand. But he did not tell his father or his mother what he had done.

Then he went down and talked with the woman; and she pleased Samson well. After some time, when he returned to get her, he turned aside to see the carcass of the lion. And behold a swarm of bees and honey were in the carcass of the lion **- (Judges 14 1-8).**

A MAN ON A MISSION

It's clear to see here, that Samson was on a mission. It's also evident in the text that wherever there is a great cause to be realised, you can be sure to face opposition. Samson could have backed down, especially in response to his parents. I am sure we can all relate! Our parents or guardians often have high hopes for us. They mean well and want to see us succeed. What do we do when the picture they have for us contrasts with the picture God has painted?

It reminds me of my story. I knew from a young age that I wanted to pursue ministry, but my parents had other plans for me – a doctor, a lawyer, but not a pastor! "There is no way of supporting yourself financially in ministry," they told me. But the conviction in me was so strong that it gave me the strength to respectfully but fervently pursue the call of God on my life.

Samson goes on to Timnah, and on his way there he meets a lion. Let's pause and consider that for a moment. Samson has gone against the advice of his parents and meets a beast on his chosen path to Timnah. I am sure you are thinking what I'm thinking. *Samson, you should have listened to your parents! If you did, you wouldn't be in this mess right now.*

CHAMPIONS HAVE VISION

Have you ever been there? You begin to feel like your decision has landed you in more trouble than you bargained for. Suffice to say, it would have been easy for Samson to look at this obstacle and turn back, defeated. But no, the text tells us, he faced that beast and a strength rose from within him, not just any strength, but the Spirit of the living God. He tore that lion apart from limb to limb!

> *Without a proper vision for your life, you run the risk of wandering aimlessly from place to place.*

The most prominent characteristic of this champion was that he started with a vision. Samson's vision was to go down to Timnah to find a wife. The name Timnah means "a place to possess or a place of inheritance." Samson set out to claim what he knew was rightfully his.

Without a proper vision for your life, you run the risk of wandering aimlessly from place to place. But just because Samson had a vision, this did not make his path smooth sailing. His vision had to withstand enemies.

KNOW YOUR PLACE OF POSSESSION

Samson could have stayed in a comfortable place and not ventured out to pursue a wife but the champion in Samson knew the calling on his life. When you know WHERE your call is, every fibre within you seeks everything you need to fulfil your destiny.

YOUR VISION WILL HAVE INTERNAL ENEMIES

Often, your vision and ideas will face opposition. It's rare that the people around you will see the big picture for your life, even those you consider nearest and dearest. Samson's parents were opposed to his plans and couldn't understand why He couldn't just stay in his own country to find a wife. The champion in Samson knew there was more to his life than the familiar and greatness was awaiting him outside his comfort zone.

This rings very true for me because as I mentioned earlier, my parents (my father especially) were strongly opposed to the idea of me being a pastor. They equated a life of ministry to a life of struggle. After all we'd encountered as a family, barely staying afloat, they wanted to me to pursue an occupation that would set me up financially.

Something happens when you face an enemy at such close proximity. I must be careful here because I'm not saying my parents were my enemies. I'm not encouraging you to regard your family as enemies either if they do not support your dreams.

What I am saying is it's important to be aware of the obstacles you will encounter along the way as you pursue your destiny. It can be confusing when you don't get support from those closest to you. I remember it created many doubts in me because even though I knew I was called to a life of ministry, it was very difficult going against my parents' wishes. It was a challenge following my calling knowing my parents were not in support of my vision for my life. It caused me to fluctuate a lot between pursuing my calling and staying with the familiar. Thoughts would go through my mind, *"Josh, they know you better than you know yourself; are you sure this is the way?"*

It affects you when the people closest to you do not approve or support the vision God has given you. When things got difficult in my ministry, I was greatly tempted to throw in the towel and abandon my dreams. It was difficult not to see myself in a negative light. My insecurities came to the surface because of the opposition to my dreams. I often asked myself, if my vision is so good, why are they opposing it? At times, it would tamper with my self-esteem and image.

> *It affects you when the people closest to you do not approve or support the vision God has given you.*

Therefore, I dare say to you that some of the obstacles we face may seem to be products of our own doing. The natural response would be to turn back and return to our starting point defeated.

I had to let my vision shout louder than the voices of my parents and my siblings. I would remind myself continually of the promise of God on my life and the vision He had given me.

Who is your internal enemy? What do you do to silence the voices that try to shout louder than your dreams?

YOUR VISION WILL HAVE EXTERNAL ENEMIES

So Samson set out to pursue his vision. As he is travelling along, the Word of God tells us that he encounters a lion. This is where it often gets interesting for people with a vision. Samson not only had to encounter the internal enemy, but he was also faced with an external enemy as well. It was one thing to face enemies within his family but another thing entirely when Samson encountered this ferocious lion. He must have really thought his vision was wrong when he encountered this beast. He must have thought about his parents and their advice. He was now in a predicament that could cost him his life. But something was up in this champion when he encountered this enemy. The Bible tells us he tore the lion from limb to limb.

When God places a vision in you, He will give you the strength and grace to sustain you on your journey. It might seem difficult at the time when we start a journey to imagine that we will have the stamina to run the course. However, God's grace is sufficient for us and we can be sure that He will back up His work.

I just love this character Samson because he was not fazed by the great lion. You can tell a champion apart from a crowd by the size of battles he is ready to fight. Samson could have turned back and run. He could have abandoned his original vision. It's easy to turn and run. But what would happen if we stared that obstacle square in the face and let the Spirit of God rise within us?

> *When God places a vision in you, He will give you the strength and grace to sustain you on your journey.*

FIGHT! I SAID FIGHT

That's what champions do. Samson faced the lion and killed it. Many of us face lions that roar against our dreams. We start out on a business venture and financial lions roar against it. Maybe yours is a ministry that God has placed on your heart but the lions of self-doubt or the lions of people's criticism roar against you. It takes a lot to recognise the lions and kill them.

FACE THE LION AND MOVE ON

What I love about Samson is that he didn't get stuck in the place where he fought the lion. Let's be honest, facing a lion is no walk in the park. It takes a lot of strength and internal fortitude. It is an exhausting and dramatic experience. Many of us recognise the lion, face it, and fight it, but we exert so much energy, we are completely drained after the fight. However, Samson fought the lion, killed it, and moved on.

Are you a tired champion? Have you lost your spark and energy? Are you a great fighter too exhausted and traumatised by the fight to move on? Are you sitting on the roadside licking your wounds?

Rise up! The fight wasn't pretty, but it was worth it. The fight was brutal, but it didn't kill you. That tells me you still have much to give.

Champions have to become well acquainted with adversity. They need to learn to navigate the before, during, and the after of the fight.

CHAPTER 5

CHARACTER STUDY ESTHER: THE ORPHANED QUEEN MOTHER

When I was young, there was a program on television called, "Queen for a Day." Several women were selected as contestants and then asked questions, which gave each woman an opportunity to show why she should be "queen." At the end of each program, one woman was selected to be "Queen for a Day." Among other prizes, her hair was done by a famous Hollywood make-up artist, and she dined at a world-famous restaurant.

Now, fast forward a few decades. We have moved on to "Queen for a Year." Choosing beauty pageants every year can be a stressful exercise; yet, a very empowering process. Contestants are selected to represent their communities, regions, states or countries. Each young woman has the opportunity to display her talent, intellect, and beauty. The contestants are narrowed down until one lucky woman is picked by the judges as the best for the year.

THE ORPHANED ONE

In reading the book of Esther, I find myself asking, "How did a young, poor, orphaned, Jewish girl manage to get herself crowned queen among all the beautiful contestants in Persia.

Esther goes by the name Hadassah. She is born like anyone else with a mother and a father. However, unfortunate circumstances leave her without parents; her mother and father tragically passed away. She is left to be raised by her uncle, Mordecai. She has no mother to glean wisdom and womanly grace from and no father to offer her security and strength. What feeble and pitiful beginnings! I can imagine how this would have made Hadassah feel. She may have gone to school and seen her friends brought to class by their parents. On open day, there would have been a sense of longing when she had no parent to sit and talk to her teachers about how well she was doing in class. Being an orphan would have made Hadassah feel less valuable and probably less entitled to succeed in life.

This young girl's background and upbringing leave much to be desired. Yet, when the time comes that a certain king is looking for a wife, Hadassah "the orphaned one" emerges from the shadows and is brought to the fore by means of a contest. Who will win the king's favour? Champions are not born; they are made.

Now it came to pass in the days of Ahasuerus (this was the Ahasuerus who reigned over one hundred and twenty-seven provinces, from India to Ethiopia), in those days when King Ahasuerus sat on the throne of his kingdom, which was in Shushan the citadel, that in the third year of his reign he made a feast for all his officials and servants--the powers of Persia and Media, the nobles, and the princes of the provinces being before him-- when he showed the riches of his glorious kingdom and the splendour of his excellent majesty for many days, one hundred and eighty days in all.
- (Esther 1:1- 4).

Take me back to those times when parties go on for half a year! The king of this nation is showing off his wealth and possessions. He is inviting everyone to celebrate with him. In a flurry of drunkenness and pride, he decides he will show off his beautiful wife Vashti as one of these prized possessions. The reigning queen defiantly refuses to take part in the king's whims. To cut a long story short, the furious king is advised to demote his defiant wife and take for himself another beautiful maiden as queen.

IN THE TIME OF TESTING CHAMPIONS WORK ON THEMSELVES

Everything around Hadassah showcases the favour bestowed on champions by God. When Hadassah is swept up into the king's quest for a wife, it is a sad and confusing time for her. Once again, Hadassah has lost her sense of belonging. She is taken away from her home. She is taken away from all she knows and trusts. She is even forced to hide her identity and her name is changed to Esther. But even in these circumstances, she finds favour. Again, we see God's familiar process of preparation.

Along with other beautiful girls, Esther goes through twelve months of beautification and preparation for royal duties. Imagine that! Twelve months getting ready for an assignment that may not even eventuate in the way she anticipates. But Esther subjects herself to this preparation.

Finally, the time comes when Esther will appear before the king. She exercises wisdom in her adornment. The other girls busy themselves putting on fancy jewellery and heavy royal clothing, but the scriptures tell us that Esther only adorns herself with what the king's eunuch suggests.

Like a love story that most women would dream of, the king is absolutely overtaken by her beauty. Esther is the king's choice!

This tells me that where we start in life does not have to determine where we will end. Esther had a rough, orphaned start, low in pedigree, but she rose to be a queen. Even in this privileged position, challenges found her.

Her circumstances did not define her, and her challenges did not stop her.

Esther could not control her early life circumstances. She lost her parents, and this must have been a traumatic time for her. And even though she was fortunate enough to have a mentor like Mordecai in her life, she must have felt somewhat disenfranchised. She must have felt like she had gotten the short end of the stick. But even in these circumstances, there is the making of a champion in Esther.

Many of us don't have control over what life throws at us. It is up to us to rise out of our circumstances and become triumphant despite our challenges. For some, it is easier to give up and throw a pity party. Esther certainly could have; she had lost not one but both parents. This would have affected her life for years to come. As if this wasn't enough, she got ripped away from her family once again when the king of the time decided he was going to find himself a replacement wife.

YOUR BEGINNING DOES NOT DETERMINE YOUR END

If you are looking at your less than ideal background, how you were raised, what you were born without or the repeated obstacles you have faced, I declare to you that your past does not determine your future. You are a champion in the making. Regardless of present circumstances, your best is yet to come.

There are countless stories throughout the course of God's Word that prove this to be so. Daniel was a captive of a tyrant king. He was called out to interpret the king's dream. After doing so successfully, he was inevitably lifted up to new levels of prosperity. This bold young man didn't forget His God, even under the most adverse of circumstances. He emerged from a hopeless situation to a promoted position.

I can share another story with you about a character called Gideon. This young man was a sorry sight to begin with. You know, one of those people who put himself down, so that no one else will have the opportunity to do so? Yes, that was Gideon. He referred to himself as, "The least in my father's house." When the angel came down to address him he was called "a mighty man of valour." The circumstances around this man are recalibrated into a story of success and triumph.

Moses, the deliverer, had humble beginnings. He was subjected at birth to the unpleasant odour of crocodiles and swamp matter, not to the warmth, love, and nurturing of a mother. Therefore, I repeat that champions are not born; they are made.

It seems to me that from the moment we are born, vulnerable and helpless, somewhere deep within God invests a championing spirit. Greatness lies dormant waiting for the right circumstances to bring forth success. I believe that those right circumstances are the challenges of life. The very stresses and struggles we love to despise.

"He came to His own, and His own did not receive Him. But as many as received Him, to them He gave the right to become children of God, to those who believe in His name." **- (John 1:11,12).**

Life may be less than ideal. Pain and obstacles may be on every side. However, those same hurts are catalysts for the emerging of the greatness in us.

> *The highway to championship includes mentors and coaches who are not jealous of you*

Esther teaches me that the highway to championship includes mentors and coaches who are not jealous of you. Rather, they are ready to push you ahead to reach your goals. The highway to championship comes with adequate preparation. Though raised by her uncle Mordecai, Esther teaches us that we can all reach our destinies if we are serious enough to invest our time, talents, and treasures.

CHAPTER 6

CHARACTER STUDY: RUTH - RESURRECTING LIFE FROM WHAT'S LEFT

The book of Ruth introduces us to how losses can devastate our lives. If we back down in the face of losses, we miss the opportunity to become instruments of victory. Ruth lost everything but, in turn, gained everything including being in the lineage of the Messiah.

We are introduced first to a woman called Naomi. Naomi was from Bethlehem and moved to Moab with her husband Elimelech and two sons, Mahlon and Kilion. Naomi later lost her husband, and she was left with her two sons.

Joy returned to Naomi's life when her two sons found wives, Ruth and Orpah. However, 10 years later, both sons died as well. Talk about a hard time, right? Thank God it is a painful story with a happy ending.

Essentially, this is a story about three women who have lost their husbands. Their hearts and lives have crumbled right before them. This is a reminder that losses and changes are hard and, unfortunately, more common than we know.

Many times, while dealing with grief, we can feel lost or forgotten. The three widows knew all too well how that felt. What do you do when you need encouragement but the person to encourage you is in the same predicament? All three ladies would have felt the sting of death. All three ladies would have wondered if any good was left in life. Naomi decided her best bet would be to return home to Bethlehem Judah.

This is the point where we see the rising of the champion in Ruth.

Ruth and Orpah were both given the blessing from Naomi to go back to their hometowns after their husbands had passed. Naomi knew she couldn't provide the women new husbands, and she wanted them to make the obvious choice for "moving forward" into other marriages if it was God's will. Orpah took the option Naomi presented. However, Ruth decided to stay with Naomi, and they headed to Bethlehem together.

"Where you go I will go, and where you stay I will stay. Your people will be my people and your God my God." **- (Ruth 1:16 NIV).**

How many times have we made choices to be in a place we "think" will give us what we want? Ruth teaches us that a champion is one who keeps her commitment even when it hurts.

Championship is a willingness to forego one's own interests and prefer others instead. Ruth stayed the course. You may be feeling overwhelmed by situations right now. You may even be at the lowest low in life but be encouraged. Your commitment to hold on to the end puts you in a class of your own.

You are a champion because you have chosen to stay in the game.

At face value, it looks like Orpah had gotten herself the better end of the stick by remaining among her own people, while Ruth was walking into unchartered territories. This shows how champions will forego their comfort when following a course, even if their GPS shows a dead end.

The Story of Ruth teaches us 3 lessons:

CHAMPIONS LET GO OF THEIR PAST

Ruth was prepared to leave her hometown and the memories of her past marriage behind.

Your past is in the tomb. Leave it behind.

Your future is in the womb. Move forward!

CHAMPIONS PAY CLOSE ATTENTION TO THEIR ASSOCIATIONS

Champions are aware that Orpahs can be setbacks to their destinies. They also know that it's the Naomis who can help shape their God-given destinies. Ruth chose to go forward with Naomi and because of that she became a champion. Through her marriage to Boaz, she was in the lineage of the Messiah.

Champions know they must invest in associations that will build them up, not tear down the good work God is doing in them.

A WALK WITH GOD IS A WALK BY FAITH.

You don't need facts and logic before you move forward. Sometimes, it's a walk in the dark that teaches me to appreciate the light inside of me.

We walk by faith, not by sight.

You can rise up.

You can stand up.

You can resurrect your life from what was left.

CHAPTER 7

CHAMPION STRATEGY 1:
CHAMPIONS ARE NOT BORN - CHAMPIONS ARE MADE

Research and surveys done in the past say only 2-5 per cent of all people succeed in life. These are startling statistics. They fuel my belief that we need to come to a place of knowledge and recognition of our champion status. It is an achievable goal done by following a set of principles that govern the traits of a champion.

You are not doomed to fail in life because of where you were born, what you have done or not done in life. You are not limited by your environment or culture. You are the master of your destiny. You determine where you will end up.

There are two schools of thought in the world,

1. **Champions are born**
2. **Champions are made**

I am inclined to agree with the latter. I believe champions are made because of the way God has designed us. Our very introduction into this world says a lot. We spend nine months in our mother's wombs and when we come out, the characteristics that surround us are ones of helplessness. We are born naked, crying, and unable to fend for ourselves. It's not a very victorious sight. It is not a scene that one would associate with a champion. Champions are not born, they are made.

As mentioned earlier, the word "champion" is defined in different ways but a simple way of putting it is "one who defies the odds and wins despite obstacles and keeps winning." Please bear that in mind. When you defy the odds and win, you are a champion. In other words, the odds may be against you, but they do not deter you. A common saying on champions is that they first win the battle and then step into the ring!

CHAPTER 8

CHAMPION STRATEGY 2:
IT TAKES A CHAMPION TO FACE ANOTHER CHAMPION

Moving back to our character study, David, we are told at this time in his life, he is seventeen years of age and tending his father's sheep. We are told that at the very same time, the military soldiers of Israel are out on the battlefield fighting against the Philistines, including Goliath. Scattered by fear of this giant, the picture we often conjure up of what a true champion looks like is shattered.

You would think military men would have some gumption! You'd think these trained warriors would have the bravado to stand their ground. But no, the Bible introduces us to David, a king and mighty man of war trapped in a shepherd's body. For years, David is faced with seemingly menial, least-of-the-least tasks. His brothers and father didn't even deem it necessary to bring him into the room when the time came to anoint the next king of Israel.

Have you ever been there? Have you experienced what it is like when those near and dear to you, who should know you the best are the ones who see the least in you?

To his family, David is no champion. He's not a king. I can just imagine what this would have done to David's self-image. I can just imagine if he had allowed it, how this oversight would have taken him off the track of God-intended greatness. He continues to tend sheep and for a time, even after his anointing, there is nothing great to report. It is only when David is faced with a challenge that the king in him comes to the fore.

We spend a lot of time despising our challenges, but I am of the school of thought that the greater the challenge I face, the greater the strength invested in me to overcome and triumph over it! It's actually a compliment when I am faced with troubles. Instead of seeing it this way though, we throw pity parties proportionate to the size of the pain. We ask questions like, "Why is God making me go through this?" "Why do these things always happen to me?" While we are asking, we miss the opportunity to see our greatness and our ability to overcome becomes harder and harder. We lament, "This is too much! I'm not cut out for this. I can't handle it." All the while, we miss God saying to us, "I trust you with this battle." He knows we can overcome it. I know this to be true because the Word of God tells me that *"No temptation has overtaken you except such as is common to man; but God is faithful, who will not allow you to be tempted beyond what you are able, but with the temptation will also make the way of escape, that you may be able to bear it* **- (1 Corinthians 10:13, NKJV).**

In other words, if God has brought you to it, He will surely bring you through it!

Too much time is wasted nursing our insecurities and the wounds of past experiences. Too much energy is spent looking at our failures and allowing them to define our future. It is safe to say that what I go through in life is proportionate to the measure of my God-given ability. Whatever the Enemy uses to destroy me, God looks at me and says, "I know you can overcome."

The enemy approached God speaking against Job, a man of faith. He was dangling catastrophic pressure and calamity as bait into the pit of demise. However, God had the confidence to say to the Devil, "Go right ahead. I know my soldier." Job lost everything: family, materials, and riches; yet, he stood to declare, "My Redeemer lives."

One of the things we need to remember is regardless of the defeated position of the devil, he does hold his own measure of power. Don't be fooled by people who tell you the devil has no power. I am in no way glorifying or giving him any undue credence, but you don't need to look far to see the influence of the devil at work. This world is in utter turmoil. Many stories of calamity after calamity are on our televisions daily. The Enemy has power friends, BUT (and this is a big but) **1 John 4:4 says**, *"Greater is He that is in us than he that is in the world."*

That word "greater" is a comparative term. To be greater, you must have a measure of greatness to be compared to. The devil is fighting a battle against us every day; albeit a losing one. However, we can all agree he is fighting. It's important to know your enemy and who you are fighting. When you understand who you are fighting, you are in a position of strength.

Suffice to say, that when we face this devil in the battleground, it is important we ditch the pity-party and make way for the champion within us to rise.

David's kingship was locked up in the battles he fought. With every battle fought, his greatness emerged: from the bear to the lion to the giant. Therefore, can we say our identities or champion natures are determined by the challenges we face? I say, yes! I see God orchestrating the fleeing of the military men of Israel from this giant so that David could fight him. If David had the other men of war around him, who would have gotten credit for the victory? There would have been a shadow of doubt about who really conquered Goliath. God isolated this young, ruddy-looking shepherd boy and set him up for an elevation in the battlefield. At the end of the day, God received all of the glory.

Does this sound familiar? Does this sound like you in any season of your life? Have all your support systems and the things that comfort you been cut off? Is there a giant of trouble taunting you and seeking to destroy everything you know about God? Look at the life of David and rejoice. It appears to me that your greatness is about to emerge.

CHAPTER 9

CHAMPION STRATEGY 3:
CHAMPIONS LOOK BEYOND THEIR ABILITIES

You come to me with a sword, with a spear, and with a javelin. But I come to you in the Name of the Lord of hosts, the God of the armies and Israel, whom you have defied. This day the Lord will deliver you into my hand, and I will strike you and take your head from you. **- (1 Samuel 17:45-46).**

If this was an action movie, I would be on the edge of my seat, heart racing and eyes glued to the screen. This is bold talk from a very young and inexperienced David! He's not only going to strike Goliath, but he's going to have his head! What I believe is happening here is that destiny is unfolding right before David's eyes. It requires him to step up to the proverbial plate and do his part to see it realised.

I would never have expected such boldness from David, simply because everyone around him seemed to be telling him he was not equipped for the task. His own brother, Eliab, made it very clear that his place was not on the battlefield but in another field with a few sheep! "Why are you even here?" he asks him.

I call it the "big brother complex."

There are times in our lives when those who we look up to and even expect to see the potential in us are the very people who look down on us. We saw it in Samson's and Joseph's lives.

David's story is a sad one because his brother does the worst thing a person can do to your self-image.

Now Eliab his oldest brother heard when he spoke to the men; and Eliab's anger was aroused against David, and he said, "Why did you come down here? And with whom have you left those few sheep in the wilderness? I know your pride and the insolence of your heart, for you have come down to see the battle
- (1 Samuel 17:28).

Eliab degrades David. It is clear also that Eliab has already formed an opinion of his younger brother. He has reduced him to nothing but insolent and prideful, totally nullifying the functionality within him. It is also apparent to me from Eliab's comments that David set a precedent that warrants his brother's comments.

People have a way of using our past to determine our future! Yet, David persists. I must be honest in saying after such a downgrading, I found myself asking what characteristics David had that made him look past his brother's comments.

It doesn't end there! King Saul, his superior, reminds David that Goliath is no child's play. "He's a man of war from youth David! You're just a youth. You have no man of war in your job description to date."

As you pass through the journey of life, you will find that those who know you best in the natural will be intent on reminding you of your level. They will remind you of your background and make sure you don't forget it! Champions do not measure themselves according to their past experiences. Champions look beyond their abilities.

I love that David's take-off point is to say to Goliath, "You come with all these earthly weapons, but I come to you with the backing power of One who is greater and more capable." David knew that on his own, his brother and

King Saul had a valid point. But what David also knew is that he and God equalled the majority.

If the battle was based on ability, David wouldn't have stood a chance. Let's be honest. Goliath was a man of war. David was not trained, and he was not experienced.

This truth applies to our battles as well. If the battle is based on our abilities and our current experiences, we stand a great chance of failing.

And if we look at the areas in which we have failed in the past, chances are we will give up before we even venture out.

It's time for us to say like David, "I don't come by myself, but I come in the name of the Lord." When we are weak, we know God is strong.

CHAPTER 10

CHAMPION STRATEGY 4:
CHAMPIONS ARE NOT MADE BY CROWDS — THEY ARE MADE WHEN THEY ARE ALONE

We like the support of people when we have challenges. But I can tell you one thing, while you may enjoy that shoulder to cry on and the support of friends and family in tough times, the true measure of the champion in you will show in your private battles. Nothing is wrong with support from friends and family in and of itself. However, we really see the shaping and moulding of the champion in us when it is just God and us in the thick of the battle.

I have an affinity for eagles; they are strange birds. They don't flock with other birds. When there is adverse weather, it is common to see flocks of birds flying in the opposite direction. But eagles wait on a rock, studying the storm. That alone is packed with power.

They study the storm's speed and potential. At the opportune time, they fly directly into the centre of it. Do you know why eagles do this? It is because they know something other birds do not? Eagles know that the turbulence of the storm pushes them higher. Eagles use the storm to enter a space that they can't reach in good weather. Now, that says something. The reward for this small piece of knowledge is a broader view of their surroundings.

What if the storm is not meant to bring us down but elevate us? What if the storm is orchestrated to bring us into a greater awareness of the power available to us in Jesus? What if the storm is a set up for a step up?

If there is something we often don't do well in our own company, it is facing trials. Yet, we could benefit from a little isolation occasionally.

Being alone gives us the time to discover our potential and strengths. It allows us to put things into perspective and to determine what is important, as well as what is not.

The children of Israel fled from the giant Goliath. This left David alone to face him. I'm sure David discovered very quickly what his actual abilities were. Had he not been aware of these, he might have made the grave mistake of going out in his name and in his strength, not in the name of the Lord.

CHAPTER 11

CONFESSIONS OF A CHAMPION

Living the life of a champion begins with what comes out of your mouth.

Say these confessions to yourself every day to build up your faith:

- I confess that I am a champion because I am a child of the Most High and a member of the body of Christ!
- My life is a manifestation of the manifold graces and perfections of God, whose glory I am, and whose presence I carry to impact and beautify my world. In the name of Jesus.
- I have full discernment and understanding of divine realities because the eyes of my spirit have been flooded with light, to know the hope of my calling and the glory of God's inheritance in the saints. In the name of Jesus.

- Daily, I experience growth, development, progress, deliverance, prosperity, and health because I am walking in the reality of who I am in Christ, taking full advantage of His grace and awesome presence in my life. In the name of Jesus.
- I am on an upward and forward journey of progress and success, positioned for glory and excellence. In the name of Jesus.
- I dwell in the secret place of the Most High and abide in His holy presence; therefore, no evil shall befall me, neither shall any plague come near my dwelling. In the name of Jesus.
- My life is beautified with God's grace and filled with His wisdom. I function excellently today through the power of the Holy Spirit who lives in me and guides me from within, piloting me from glory to glory. In the name of Jesus.
- I function in the dominion of the Spirit, having been enthroned over Satan, the principalities of darkness, and all negative circumstances. In the name of Jesus.
- I am not ordinary, for greater is He that is in me, than he that is in the world! In the

name of Jesus. Blessed be God. Hallelujah!
- I affirm that I am full of the wisdom of God, like David, for Christ is made unto me wisdom!
- That wisdom is in my heart and in my mouth today! In the name of Jesus.
- I function in it. I am guided by it, and I am growing in it daily as I continually meditate on the Word and fellowship with the Holy Spirit. In the name of Jesus.
- The knowledge of God's Word in my spirit puts me over and gives me the victory over giants, victory over fear, and victory over every opposing voice today! In the name of Jesus.
- Fear, sickness, poverty, and death have no place in me because I live by faith in the Word of God, which is my recipe for total success, victory, prosperity, and divine health. In the name of Jesus.
- The Word of God is the rock that slays every giant in my life. It is the source of my life. It is living and active in me today! In the name of Jesus.
- I experience the transforming power of the Word in my finances, health, family, and in everything that concerns me. In the name of Jesus.

- My life is upgraded today by the power of God's Word. In the name of Jesus!
- I am inspired by today's possibilities and tomorrow's potentials. In the name of Jesus.
- Through the Word of God, my mind is renewed and my spirit is enlightened to see my future: the greatness, success, victory, and prosperity, which God has ordained to be my day-to-day experience in Christ! In the name of Jesus. Blessed be God. Hallelujah!

CONCLUSION

When I look at my life and the number of lives that have been impacted by this ministry, I am amazed by the love of God. God used my humble, meagre beginnings as a little boy. It would have been easier to give up than go through some of those painful experiences.

I often meet people who have settled for average lives. Average then becomes the standard measure.

Perhaps we can learn from the following story of how mother eagle trains its young ones to fly. We all know that eagles are called majestic birds. We marvel as we see how they master the winds and mount up on higher altitudes in stormy weather. But reaching this level of fortitude comes as a result of lots of painful training.

Eagles make their nests in high altitudes and in trees where the wild animals cannot reach to devour the eggs and their eaglets. When the time comes to teach the eaglets to fly, the mother eagle takes on what we might perceive to be quite a cruel position in the lives of its young. But mama knows it's the only way her babies will become champions.

The mother eagle begins by rattling the comfortable nest as if to say to its young ones "there is no time for a comfort zone." Then, it pushes the young eaglets out of the nest. Yes, a painful and shocking process, but one of the most important stages in the life of an eagle.

When the nest is destroyed by the mother eagle it then carries the young ones to high altitudes in its talons and lets go of the untrained, naive, and vulnerable eaglets in an attempt to make them exercise their wings.

The ability to fly is almost never realised in the first lesson. But that exposure marks the end of "average" in the life of the baby eagle.

I don't know where life has placed you. You may be facing what seems like insurmountable odds. Life may be throwing you what seems like unfair curveballs intent to cancel you out of the game. But I encourage you to let the champion in you rise.

We are programmed by society to expect comfort. If it's hard, it's not for you! If you have to struggle for it, it must not be your portion! I challenge this thinking! I hope you can see from the many examples placed before us, that the

CONCLUSION

challenges in our lives bring forth greater victories than the comforts of our lives can.

Champions are not born, they are made!

See you at the TOP!

www.ingramcontent.com/pod-product-compliance
Lightning Source LLC
Chambersburg PA
CBHW032044290426
44110CB00012B/951